MEDITATION FOR BEGINNERS

7 Incredible and Easy Ways to Still Your Mind, Hear the Voice of Your Intuition and Trust Your Heart through Meditation

Nicolas Knoll

Copyright © 2015, All Rights Reserved

Table Of Contents

Introduction 4
Benefits of Meditation 7
   The ultimate meditation benefit 11
Chapter 1 - Active Meditation 14
   Stage I – Chaotic Breathing (takes around 10 minutes) 16
   Stage II – Catharsis (10 minutes) 17
   Stage III – Making the 'Hoo!' sound (10 minutes) .. 19
   Stage IV – Freezing (15 minutes) 20
   Stage V – Celebration (15 minutes) 22
   Some precautions you must take 23
Chapter 2 - Running or Swimming Meditation 24
   How to practice running/swimming meditation? 25
Chapter 3 - Breathing Meditation 28
   What is it about? 28
   3 methods of breathing meditation 30
Chapter 4 - Whirling Meditation 35
   How to practice this meditation? 35
Chapter 5 - Dynamic Dancing Meditation 38
   How to do it? 38
Chapter 6 - Meditating with Humming and Hands 42
   How to do it? 42
   The couples' variation 44

Chapter 7 - Sitting Meditation 46
  How to do it?...47
Conclusion 49

INTRODUCTION

Meditation, the word often brings up images of otherworldly Hindu priests or exotic Tibetan monks repeatedly chanting religious verses somewhere in the upper Himalayas! This notion may have been considered true several decades ago, but not anymore.

The word meditation has different meanings when talked about in different contexts. By definition, it is any practice that helps you train your mind or induce a certain mode of consciousness, for either accomplishing some benefit or for simply acknowledging your mind's content without getting identified with it. On the other hand, it may simply be practiced not as any means, but an end in itself.

Practicing meditation can help molding our consciousness in a manner that we experience and enjoy feelings like internal energy, stillness of mind, deep relaxation, concentration, patience, love and compassion, apart from gaining the ability to trust and follow our heart and hear the voice of our intuition.

Over the years, meditation has percolated down from the mountains and has reached the masses across continents, owing to our increasing awareness of our stress levels and the dire need of detaching ourselves from the frantic lifestyles.

In this detailed guide on 7 different ways of using meditation to enjoy many of its benefits, I'll take you through the specific techniques that have been developed and honed over several decades or centuries. A large majority of these have their origins in Asia, where meditation actually comes from.

Don't worry, I'll not ask you to pack your bags and head to Himalayas! Nor am I going to make you walk over bed of burning coal, or stand on your head! None of that! All that I'm going to do is provide you with some simple meditation techniques that you can easily practice within the four walls of your own home or somewhere outside, anytime you want.

However, before we begin, you need to make one promise to me. Promise me that you'll gather enough determination and firm up your mind to stick to these techniques no matter what. Although it's not an unachievable task, you're bound to face several distractions along the way. Hence, it's important for you to make this psychological commitment before you begin. Also, keep an open mind for the new techniques that you're going to learn. Some of them may seem funny or awkward, or don't make much sense, but they do work, I can promise you that.

Telling you from my personal experience, I feel no hesitation in claiming that meditation is by far the best thing that I've ever done for myself. I simply love it! It helps me silence my mind, concentrate better and de-stress easily. However, beware! Despite meditation being very simple in terms of its concept, it does take some time to learn to focus your mind and ease it into the relaxation mode. So, be patient.

The purpose of this book is to give you a detailed information on some of the best and most powerful meditation techniques and practices you can follow to get the maximum benefits from them. These will be suitable for beginners who have never done meditation before, but also for people who have already incorporated meditation into their lives and now want to try some cool new ways to meditate.

BENEFITS OF MEDITATION

We all know how hectic our present-day lives are. The challenges we face each day can pile up a lot of stress. As explained in the introduction section, meditation can play a very key role in helping you lead a productive, fulfilling and healthy lifestyle.

Following is a list of the most popular psychological, physiological, emotional and other health related benefits provided by meditation. Please note that this list is not exhaustive by any means!

Boost to immunity levels – Meditation provides spontaneous relaxation to the human body and boosts the production of white blood cells. A spike in white blood cells' count is usually related to improved resistance towards disease-causing viruses.

Independence from pain killers – A study carried out by researchers in Montréal in the year 2010 revealed that meditation can actually thicken that part of the human brain which regulates pain. Such thickening of the brain automatically reduces the person's sensitivity to pain.

Better focus – Meditation on its own requires tremendous focus, and this ability ripples down to other areas of life. Hence, people who meditate regularly often feel improvement in their work lives as well.

Reduced muscle tension – Relaxed muscles are a direct result of meditation. And the reduced muscle tension makes a person full of vigor, strength, energy and vitality.

Better sex – Every sexual encounter makes the human body release certain happy hormones, known as endorphins. These hormones' production is critical for the accomplishment of orgasm. A mind relaxed through regular meditation, produces large quantities of endorphins, hence leading to better sexual performance.

Combats hot flashes in menopausal women – Women going through menopause are often advised to shut out the feeling of body awareness. No woman feels comfortable embracing such uncontrollable body changes that mark the start of a new phase in her life. Practicing meditation at such a time can help you significantly in dealing with such inevitable changes. Scientific studies have proven that women who undergo relaxation therapies like meditation handle menopause symptoms far better than others.

Decrease in blood pressure – Whenever a person's body is in a relaxed state, it doesn't respond easily to the stress-causing hormones. This leads to a decrease in blood pressure.

Better fertility levels – Scientific research has revealed that women's fertility levels are at peak when their bodies are relaxed. Such relaxation is actually the USP of meditation.

Better emotional balance – People who meditate regularly have a more positive outlook towards life, compared to non-meditating individuals. Past events and circumstances often make people lead very emotional lives, causing feelings of low self-esteem and self-denial. Regular meditation can help in letting go of the bitter past and in making a fresh start.

Higher job satisfaction – Physical and mental relaxation are key to satisfactory work lives. Meditating on a regular basis can help achieving relaxation at both these levels and make you more productive at your workplace.

Ability to look at the bigger picture – Meditating on a regular basis helps people in focusing their energies on bigger issues and reduces stress arising from petty issues. Gaining such ability is very critical as it contributes to personal growth and saves a lot of time that would otherwise have been spent on resolving irrelevant and small issues.

More willpower – Meditation helps you connect with your true abilities and makes you determine to never give up. You get the willpower to make every situation work, no matter how complex it may be. When you do this regularly, you automatically start living a fulfilled life with a sense of personal achievement.

Aids mental growth – Meditation is often associated with the ability of grasping information easily. So whether you're an employee or student, you'll experience tremendous mental growth and will be on top of every situation. Meditation also improves the mental and physical alertness levels, which in turn assist the brain in grasping important information and use it effectively to lead a positive life.

Works as a cure for insomnia – Sleep related disorders or insomnia are often associated with stress. Having a relaxed state of mind can help you create a proper sleeping routine and more importantly stick to it. Furthermore, a person who meditates regularly doesn't take very long to fall asleep once she/he hits the sack. What more, he/she enjoys a more sound and un-disturbed sleep!

Can relieve IBS (Irritable Bowel Syndrome) – Meditating for 1 to 2 hours every day has such effect on the body that IBS symptoms like bloating, diarrhea and constipation get relieved easily over a period of time.

A calm and composed attitude – Meditating people usually have calm and composed attitude as against the people who don't meditate. This is a direct result of their relaxed mind, which helps them analyze and study a situation before commenting on or reacting to it. Non-meditating individuals usually take impulsive decisions without paying heed to the consequences.

Better relationships – How a person relates to the people around him/her undergoes a major positive change if he/she maintains a regular meditation routine. Meditation automatically provides a feeling of contentment, which gets translated into happiness at a deeper level. A happy person bonds more easily with people around him/her than someone who is always disturbed and/or sad.

Better heart health – Your cardiovascular system or heart is the automatic beneficiary of reduced stress. Meditation has the ability to improve your body's internal functions like breathing and blood circulation by counteracting feelings of anxiety, arousal and stress.

Slowing down of neurodegenerative diseases - A pilot study carried out by researchers in Israel revealed that the brain changes caused as a result of stress reduction and meditation may help significantly in slowing down the worsening of age-related cognitive disorders such as Alzheimer's disease.

THE ULTIMATE MEDITATION BENEFIT

While practicing meditation on a regular basis can undoubtedly improve your life as discussed above, there is one benefit that is in my opinion the most valuable of them all.

I think you'll agree that we want awesome things and experiences in our lives, and most of all we want to become amazing people. The kind of people that bring joy to wherever they go, that are a source of inspiration to others, and that wake up happy each day knowing deeply within their hearts that they are living life to its fullest capacity. We all want to live that fulfilling life.

But do you know what it is that makes you truly happy, what moves you, what makes you sleep less each night and wake up early because of the excitement for everything that you're going to do that day? Do you know what it's like to live a purposeful life? Knowing what your purpose is at any particular moment, being aware of it, leads you toward a fulfilling life.

How do you find all that out, you may wonder?! I'll tell you.

You find that out by **looking within**.

Looking within and getting to know yourself better is what brings you to discovering your purpose, your mission, what it is that you love and want to do, what will truly make you happy and bring you joy and fulfillment in your life.

Great news is that meditation helps you discover exactly that. It gets you to look within and really get to know yourself.

- You'll discover what an amazing person you are.

- You will start looking for happiness from the inside, and not from the outside sources like money or other people.

- You will find happiness within you.

- You will become a better version of yourself.

- You will still your mind, hear the voice of your intuition and start following your heart.

That in my opinion is the ultimate meditation benefit.

Now let's get onto the 7 ways of meditating for beginners. I'll try to explain everything in an easy way for you to follow. It is recommended that you go through the whole book first, and then try the methods that appeal to you the most.

Chapter 1 - Active Meditation

Also commonly referred to as dynamic meditation, this way of meditating is quite opposite to the way meditation is perceived by many all over the world, especially in the west. People often relate meditation to silence, the absence of effort and activity. However, active meditation, as evident from its name is full of activity!

Without wasting any time, let's get straight to how you must perform this meditation. It is divided into 5 different stages. Please note, you may find the activities detailed in these stages quite funny, especially if you're new to this form of meditation. However, great deal of benefits, both mental and physical, await you if you practice them seriously.

First you'll want to find a quiet place where nobody will disturb you and you won't disturb anybody. This is going to be intense. ;)

Before you begin you can do some stretches of the abdominal region by leaning backwards (while standing straight) as much as you can, with your arms pointing away from your chest to the sides, and your mouth wide open (as if you're yawning). Make sure that you breathe deeply so that your belly expands with every breath.

Also do the opposite movement where you lean forward with your fingers touching the ground in front of your feet and your knees bent slightly. You should feel your belly expanding easily with every breath.

You can also stretch your neck, shoulders and even your jaw by doing simple stretch exercises. Lean your head to the sides, left and right, in circles, open your mouth and move your jaw around, and don't forget to breathe calmly and deeply.

This may be a little bit uncomfortable but that is expected. These exercises will release some muscle tension in this key region of your core, your neck and shoulders. They are a good 'warm up' for what you'll be doing in the next five stages.

These stretches can help with active meditation but they are entirely optional and should be avoided if you have medical back issues.

It's best to do this meditation while standing straight. Relax your whole body and wear a comfortable clothes. It may help if you are barefoot for the next five stages for being more grounded and getting better results.

Note that the times I've put in parenthesis are optimal and merely suggestions. There is no need to look at your watch for every activity. It is best to give yourself one hour for this to have enough room to complete each phase. As you do this, you should learn to feel when you're ready for the next phase.

Let's begin!

STAGE I – CHAOTIC BREATHING (TAKES AROUND 10 MINUTES)

Breathe slowly and deeply at first. Then, when you feel you're ready, start breathing heavily in and out via your <u>nose</u> and concentrate on the exhalation aspect of your breathing. You should feel your breath going deep into your lungs and your chest expanding with every inhalation.

Next try breathing as fast as possible, ensuring that your breath goes in really deep, so much that you feel a tingling sensation in your pelvic floor. Make sure you do this as correctly as you can without stiffening up your body. Your shoulders and neck should stay relaxed throughout the movement.

Continue this activity until the time you can feel your whole body breathing, allowing every breath to be as chaotic as possible. You'll feel energy moving through your body, and actually moving your body. Allow such body movements to occur and utilize them to build even more energy.

Don't shy away from employing your body and arms in a natural manner to help this energy rise, without slowing down through the movement. Feel it building up inside you, and don't let it go.

SIGNIFICANCE

Such chaotic breathing is meant to create a type of chaos inside your repressed system. As a result, it helps you release all your repressed emotions. Not only will such chaotic breathing provide you with more oxygen, it'll make you feel more alive!

The more repressed your system is the more shallow your breathing will be. That's why it's important to breathe as deeply as possible. At the end of this stage you might start crying or laughing for no obvious reason to you at all. That is good since you're releasing trapped emotions in your body.

The reason why you are breathing through the nose and not through your mouth is because breathing through the mouth gets the oxygen straight to the chest and it doesn't stimulate the brain like breathing through the nose does. Stimulating the brain by breathing this way is very important for getting out of your head and into your body and changing your state. All this leads you to the Catharsis phase.

STAGE II – CATHARSIS (10 MINUTES)

During this stage or a phase of active meditation, you must follow your body closely. Give it complete freedom and control to express whatever's there inside you. Allow your inner emotions to explode!

As explained above, you'll need to let your body take control and let go of all the emotions that must be thrown out. Get out of your head and move the energy into your body. Don't refrain from going mad! It may sound funny to you initially, but believe me it works!

Jump, kick, sing, shout, scream, shake, laugh, cry, tremble, throw yourself around and do whatever you feel like doing to ease yourself up! Don't hold anything back and keep your entire body in motion throughout this stage.

Perhaps putting up a little act may help you get started!

One important point – while you're inducing catharsis, don't allow your mind to interfere in whatever's happening. You need to completely support your body while it's purging all the emotions.

SIGNIFICANCE

As you may have figured out by now, this movement is all about becoming <u>consciously insane</u>. You express whatever comes to your mind, without any resistance. Simply put, you let the emotions flow in an unhindered manner. Don't worry, if it seems forced initially.

We've gotten so used to pretending and acting that our real emotions don't surface easily. You must give yourself some time. Continue with this movement and you'll soon touch the places inside you where you've repressed so many things for so long. Expressing them will make you so light and unburdened. It'll be like a new birth! A liberating feeling!

The point is not to lose yourself but to <u>consciously</u> lose yourself. Experience and feel every emotion that comes out but at the same remember to separate your mind and be the witness to these feelings, thoughts and changes that you're going through. That is the key to successful meditation!

Once you've thrown out every emotion, you'll become vacant and ready for the next stage.

STAGE III – MAKING THE 'HOO!' SOUND (10 MINUTES)

Yes you read that right! Trust me, this is not the only funny thing you'll be doing. On a serious note, having felt the first-hand effects of all these techniques, I can state with great confidence that they do work. So, stay with me here!

Getting back to the activity, leave/drop your neck and shoulders, allowing them to relax. Now raise both your arms as high as possible, without locking your elbows. Keeping your arms in such a raised position, start jumping up and down and shouting – hoo! hoo! hoo! as deeply as you can. This sound must ideally come right from the bottom region of your belly. However, don't worry if you can't feel it happening that way in the beginning.

Make sure that every time you land on the ground, the flat area of your feet, especially the heels, touch the floor entirely. When they do, let the sound produced hammer deep into your body's sex center. Give your all to this movement and continue doing it until you feel completely exhausted.

SIGNIFICANCE

After emptying yourself in the previous stage, your body will become blank and able enough to meditate and transform. This is achieved by making the sound 'hoo!' Every sound has its own meaning. Hindus chant the word 'aum' which helps them strike their heart center. Sufis use the 'hoo' sound. When you make this sound loudly, it strikes deep at the sex center of your body (your pelvic floor).

This 'hoo' sound will have a hammering effect only if you had emptied your repressed emotions in the previous step. Avoid chanting this word unless you have completed the previous two stages successfully. Performing this step successfully helps you go with the flow of energy inside you. You'll feel this energy moving up your spine. And the higher it goes, the higher you'll feel yourself moving with it.

Please note, the above detailed three stages or steps are cathartic. They aren't meditation literally, but prepare you for the real deal. They set you up for the jump that you'll experience in the next stage.

STAGE IV – FREEZING (15 MINUTES)

Stop and freeze in whatever position you're in and wherever in the meditation or activity area you are.

Refrain from rearranging your body in any particular way. Indulging in any physical movement, including coughing, sneezing, yawning etc. may dissipate the flow of energy, thereby compromising the entire movement. If you feel like sneezing or coughing, hold it as much as you can.

Just allow your body to "die", so that it can move the energy inside you, in an upward flow.

While you're in a frozen position, objectively view everything that's currently happening with you. Remember to witness everything that's happening!

SIGNIFICANCE

When you stop and freeze, allowing the energy inside you to flow upwards without any hindrance, your body will achieve a state of 'silence' that is equivalent to disappearance. It'll be a bodiless feeling. It's important that you just become a witness to such silence, observing whatever's happening.

This is where meditation will happen and change something significant inside you.

You'll never be the same again! This is because it's not an experience that you come back from, but a growth that changes and transforms you completely from within and without.

Please keep in mind that you'll not be able to achieve this state unless you've successfully completed the first three stages.

Stage V – Celebration (15 minutes)

In this stage, you simply need to celebrate your transformation. Celebrate it with dance and music, and express whatever is inside of you! Don't avoid carrying this new aliveness with you for the remaining part of the day. You don't need to be a professional dancer to feel good about this act. Avoid forcing it. Rather allow it to flow freely through you. The music helps with this.

To give you an example, the music I found to be very liberating and meditative for me was from famous 'Where the Hell Is Matt' videos on Youtube, both 2008. and 2012. versions. I also really like Hans Zimmer compositions, some classical music, and other music genres as well. You can of course listen to anything that you like as long as it puts you in great emotionally uplifting mood. It's a good idea to find the best music and have it ready before starting this meditation.

It's important that you practice this last phase in a festive mood, as there's nothing serious about it. All you're doing is playing with your bioenergy, enabling it to move in its natural way.

Significance

This step is all about celebrating the life energy inside you and allowing it to flow naturally, without any pretension. Simply celebrate the new, better you. If you've been able to watch yourself during this whole process then you have witnessed the changes and the emotions that you've gone through.

You have looked deep within your soul and now you know yourself better than before. This will lead you toward a more fulfilling life. There are many other benefits of this as discussed before.

Some Precautions You Must Take

Dynamic or active meditation must be practiced only at a safe place, avoiding hard surfaces where one may be prone to falls. A large hall or room having thick carpeting, where you can move freely, may be ideal.

You can also practice this meditation outdoors during the morning hours, on well-tended and soft lawns. It works pretty well if you practice it in a group.

Furthermore, active meditation works better if you do it empty stomach and it's alright to open up your eyes in between to figure out your exact location!

Chapter 2 - Running or Swimming Meditation

You must be wondering how can your everyday habit of running/jogging or swimming be termed as a type of meditative routine?! And if it's really true, how come you never experienced any enlightenment?!

I'm not a Buddhist, nor do I take any religion very seriously for that matter. However, this doesn't take away from the fact that I've always been intrigued by the Buddhist philosophy; even the Western forms it has assumed over the past several decades. A person's ability to detach himself/herself from his/her emotions, silencing the chatter inside his/her mind and tapping into his/her creative subconscious; not to forget the ability to develop compassion for other people – all these things sound very appealing, even if they're viewed objectively, free from any religious interpretation.

So when someone enlightened me about the meditation potential of running and jogging, I was more than curious to find out more! What I experienced as a result of my curiosity is something inexplicable! Let me share the technique with you too!

Note that this can also be applied to crisp walking, biking or even canoeing if that's what you prefer. It can actually be applied to any activity that incorporates rhythmic movement of your body while keeping your heart rate within aerobic levels, allowing you to clear and focus your mind at the same time.

How to practice running/swimming meditation?

Before moving to the exact process, it's important that you find something to focus on (or your focal point). You may choose to focus on either of the following:

- Your footsteps, or strokes/kicks if you're swimming

- The up-and-down motion of your abdomen with the air entering and exiting your body, through breathing

- Any particular mental image

- The present moment, its environment and everything you can experience and sense inside it

- The feeling throughout your body as you run/swim, with each one of your body parts working in tandem to push you ahead

- The feeling of air that your nose is breathing in and out

The exact routine

Once you've figured out your focal point, take the following steps:

1) Start by running/swimming/riding slowly, ideally somewhere in nature or in a place where there's not much traffic.

2) Give yourself around 15 to 20 minutes to relax. This'll help you get into the desired zone. Many times I brainstorm different ideas related to different projects when I'm jogging. Over a period of time, I've discovered that it takes at least this much time (15 to 20 minutes) to feel the ideas flowing freely.

3) Once ready, start directing your mind towards the focal point you had decided.

4) Now, try your best to maintain your focus on that one particular thing. There's no need to engage in a constant inner dialogue, repeating the thing you're trying to focus on, or anything else. What's important is that you stretch this activity as long as possible without getting disturbed by any thoughts. You must feel and become the thing you're focusing on, without the need of repeating any words inside your head. It has probably happened to you spontaneously before and you just didn't notice it.

5) Gently guide back your attention to the focal point whenever your mind strays here and there. This may happen every few seconds initially, but you'll learn to master it over a period of time. It's important that you avoid attaching any feelings of frustration or negativity to such frequent wandering of your mind.

6) Continue doing this as long as you find it possible and enjoyable. Most people are able to maintain their interest for no more than 5 to 10 minutes in the

beginning. But, don't worry. You'll be able to focus for longer durations with time.

WHAT'S THE WHOLE POINT OF DOING ALL THIS?

You may be wondering what's the purpose or goal behind maintaining such focus while running, swimming or jogging?! To tell you the truth:

There's no goal!

Yes, you read that right. You do it simply because it enables you to explore your true self. And more importantly because it feels good. If it helps you relax, that's a benefit. In case you feel more creative and attentive after meditating this way, that's also a benefit. But, my understanding of it is that there's no specific end that you must strive for. And that itself is a great change from everything we do in our day-to-day lives!

When you practice this way of meditation every day, you'll soon come to a point where the runner/swimmer in you will disappear, and only the running/swimming will remain. Your soul, mind and body will start functioning in harmony, and you'll experience an inner orgasm all of a sudden. The feeling can't be described in words!

Chapter 3 - Breathing Meditation

This way of meditating has been considered one of the golden means of practicing meditation, as you don't need to perform any extreme activities - neither related to abstinence, nor indulgence. It's guaranteed to work, regardless of your religious background or beliefs. Breathing meditation has been working for over 2500 years, and continues to provide amazing and miraculous results. In fact, many experts consider breathing meditation to be the meditation method of the future, owing to its extreme simplicity and powerful results. It fits in very easily into the complicated lifestyles we lead in the 21st-century when our free time is almost equal to zero.

What is it about?

Breathing meditation is all about watching your breath with complete awareness. That's all! Nothing more, nothing less! Just watch and concentrate on your breath as you take it in and let it go every moment, each day.

Breathing is by far the most significant process performed by our bodies. No one can exist without continuous breathing, even for one single moment. It's so significant that nature has automated it in all living beings. You don't have to remind yourself to breathe, ever. It just happens. Just like other vital processes of our bodies, such as digestion of food, pumping of the heart, blood circulation etc., breathing is also something that happens by itself.

Hundreds of different meditation techniques have been developed in the past, revolving around breathing. In fact, majority of meditation techniques taught by spiritual schools throughout the world are focused on breathing. The reason why breathing is given so much importance and love in the meditation circles is because it is far from the mere act of inhaling oxygen and excelling carbon dioxide. If you look closely, breathing actually functions as a bridge between our true self and our body. Sounds complicated?! Don't worry, I'll make it easier!

We breathe continuously, almost without a pause right from the moment we set foot into this world, till the moment we pass away. Breathing is what connects our body and soul. So, when you meditate on this important body activity, you're automatically able to connect to your true self.

In breathing meditation, you just need to be constantly aware of your breath. Regardless of the action you're currently involved in, just be constantly aware of your body's breathing process. Watch it as it comes into your body, and then goes out of it. Don't try controlling it. Whether it's shallow or deep, let it be.

3 METHODS OF BREATHING MEDITATION

As mentioned earlier, there are all sorts of methods of doing breathing meditation, however, I'll share with you the ones that I've found most effective. How they're different from each other is the points they make you focus your attention on while breathing. Initially, you may learn and master these methods in some silent and separate room, just to avoid any embarrassment! But later, you can practice them at any public place without any difficulty.

MEDITATING ON THE BREATH PASSING THROUGH YOUR NOSTRILS

An important type of breathing meditation, this one can be practiced easily anywhere and anytime without anyone noticing what you're doing.

Have you ever observed your breathing closely and felt that soothing and cooling sensation delivered by the air entering into your body via the nostrils? Try experiencing it right now as you read. Whether you can acknowledge it at this moment or not, the inhaled air via nostrils always produces such cooling sensation inside it. Although this coolness is very slight; slight enough to the extent of being almost unnoticeable, it exists nevertheless.

This technique of breathing meditation involves focusing your attention on this cooling sensation. Just like the act of breathing, this cooling sensation also gets produced on its own, as a natural byproduct of inhaling air. You can accomplish a meditative state of mind by focusing all your attention on this sensation.

How to do it?

Seat yourself comfortably in a peaceful and comfortable place. Now, close your eyes and breathe deeply a few times. Thereafter, start observing the breath passing through your nostrils and the comforting cooling sensation it delivers inside your nose (during inhalation). Continuously engaging your mind in observing this coolness will relax your mind. It'll work as if there's an air conditioner fitted inside your mind!

Continue this meditation for at least 15 to 20 minutes, until you find yourself going into a deep meditative state.

The quality of your meditation will improve slowly over a period of time, and will deliver an enhanced state of self-awareness. Although simple, this is a highly powerful meditation method you can do anytime when you need to quickly de-stress.

Belly watching breathing meditation

We all have seen the images of the pot-bellied laughing Buddha! He's an integral part of the Japanese tradition, and is in quite contrast to the conventional Buddha image that comes to mind (of a serene enlightened person). Although the laughing Buddha seems funny, there's a subtle message in its depiction. This message pertains to the important role that belly plays in meditation.

Our belly features a point of consciousness that's actually the center of our bodies (right below the belly button or navel). You can easily achieve a meditative state of mind by focusing your attention on this center. This meditative state comes in the form of choice-less awareness!

Such 'belly watching breathing meditation' requires focusing your attention on the breathing activity that can be sensed around the belly region. Your belly moves in up and down direction whenever you breathe. This belly movement happens continuously, just like breathing. Focusing attention on this movement makes you get into a meditative state of mind. Let's learn how.

How to do it?

Find some peaceful and quiet place where you can practice this meditation without any disturbance. Now close your eyes and then take deep breath a few times. Focusing your attention on the belly region, observe how it moves upwards and downwards with every breath. Avoid getting distracted by anything external or internal.

If you do this continuously, you'll experience your unwanted thoughts disappearing gradually from your mind. After sometime, you'll enter a life state of higher awareness. Witness the changes happening inside your body while meditating this way, without identifying with any of them. 15 to 20 minutes is ample time to practice this meditation. Once through, come out of the meditative state by stopping observing the belly movement.

By practicing this meditation daily basis, you'll soon become more aware and connected to your inner self.

MEDITATING BY OBSERVING YOUR BREATHING LIKE THE FLOW OF A RIVER

One of the basic forms of breathing meditation, this one is entirely about observing your breath as it enters and exits your body.

How to do it?

Just like the earlier two methods, you must find a peaceful place for yourself and sit down comfortably. Now close your eyes and take few deep breaths. Closely observe your breathing, following it attentively as it travels through your body and then exits it.

You must observe it as if it's a river. Think of a flowing river and you observing the water flow from the banks. There's no need to be concerned about the quality of water, the speed with which it's flowing or whether there are any ripples or not. You just need to observe the river without getting involved in the flowing act.

Just like a river, observe your breath entering and exiting your body, without getting attached to it. You may get distracted by all sorts of thoughts, but bring yourself back.

Soon, you'll enter a meditative state of mind, wherein your mind will become still. You'll be able to recognize and acknowledge your true self. And bask in its glory!

Chapter 4 - Whirling Meditation

There are different kinds of dancing meditation routines, and whirling meditation is one of the important and effective ones among them. It is one of the oldest and extremely powerful dancing meditation techniques that has depth enough to completely transform you into a different person, just by one single experience. But it may not the best for beginners to start out with.

While performing this meditation, it's important that you keep your eyes open. You must feel as if your inner being has become the center point and your entire body is a wheel, moving around this center.

How to practice this meditation?

Avoid taking any fluids or solids for 3 hours prior to starting whirling. Put on loose clothing and go bare feet if possible. This meditation is performed in two different phases – whirling and resting.

Whirling (Phase I)

Whirling doesn't have any fixed time, and can go on for several hours. Nevertheless, it is recommended that you continue doing it for minimum 1 hour to fully experience the energy whirlpool field.

It's normally done by rotating in anticlockwise direction, keeping the left arm low, palm downwards, and the right arm high, palm upwards. If you feel discomfort whirling in anticlockwise direction, feel free to switch to clockwise movement.

Allow your body to go soft, keeping your eyes open and unfocused, enabling the images to appear flowing and blurred. Stay silent.

Rotate slowly during the initial 15 minutes, and thereafter gradually increase the speed over the next 30 minutes. The idea is to allow whirling to take over your body, so that you turn into an energy whirlpool.

A time will come when you'll be whirling so fast that it may be impossible to stay upright. At this time, your body will fall naturally. Please note that this fall shouldn't be your decision, else you may try arranging the landing position in advance. If you're whirling correctly, your body will turn so soft that it'll fall on its own. And when you do fall down, you'll land on the surface softly, with the earth absorbing every bit of your energy.

RESTING (PHASE II)

The second part of this dancing meditation begins after the fall. When you fall down, immediately roll on to your stomach in a manner that your navel touches the floor directly. You can lie on your back if you feel uncomfortable lying on your stomach. It's important for you to feel your body getting blended with the Earth, just like a newborn presses himself/herself to his/her mother's breasts naturally. Don't open your eyes yet and remain in silent and passive mode for another 15 minutes at least.

Once you're through with the whirling dance meditation movement, stay as inactive and quiet as possible. Many people new to whirling experience nausea during its practice. However, such feeling disappears quickly on its own in a matter of 2 to 3 days. Discontinue dancing meditation for some time and see a qualified doctor if the nausea feeling persists.

You release a lot of tension while performing such dancing meditation. Many people even get path-breaking creative insights during the movement.

Tension is nothing but trapped energy, and whirling dance movement is an excellent way to release this energy and to make it move. When you feel free inside your body, your mind expands and your heart opens up, setting your spirit free. When you lie still after performing the dance, your physical activity comes to a halt and every bit of released energy starts travelling inwards, right down to the subtle layers of your being. By using the whirling meditation technique, you can make the dynamic movements of dance affect the very core or the roots of your being, setting free the transforming feelings of positivity and joy.

Chapter 5 - Dynamic Dancing Meditation

This type of meditation is a blend of the active meditation technique that I explained earlier and the dancing meditation. The best time to practice it is late afternoon or at the sunset time and barefoot if possible.

I'll soon go into the details of how to meditate this way, but before that, please know that when doing it, you must get fully immersed in the dancing and shaking part of it (during the initial two stages). These help in melting away the rock-like bodies we possess nowadays, and the stiffness which is a byproduct of blocking and repression of the energy flow inside the body.

Once set free, this energy can flow easily, dance and transform into pure joy and bliss. The last two stages of this meditation method cause the energy to flow upwards, in a vertical direction, leading to pure silence.

Such dynamic dancing meditation is highly effective in letting everything go, unwinding and de-stressing at the end of the day.

How to do it?

As mentioned above, this meditation method is divided into 4 different stages as follows:

Stage I – Loosening up and shaking (15 minutes)

Allow your entire body to loosen up and shake properly. You'll feel the energy is moving upwards right from your feet. Don't bother if it makes you go everywhere in the practice area. The point is to become the shaking. Furthermore, your eyes may stay closed or open abruptly every now and then during the movement.

The point is to let your body vibrate and let the shaking support and amplify this vibration. You can also make a simple, deep and continuous 'um' sound as you do this, as it helps with the vibration.

Stage II – Free-form dancing (15 minutes)

Let your body dance anyway it feels comfortable. Don't hold back and allow your entire body to move and dance in a free-form manner, as it wishes. Try not to think, just act.

Stage III – The stillness (15 minutes)

Close your eyes and stay still wherever you are in the practice area, regardless of whether you're standing or sitting or even laying on the floor. Try witnessing everything that is happening there, inside as well as outside.

STAGE IV – FEEL THE SILENCE (15 MINUTES)

Lie down with your eyes closed and rest while being aware of the silence. Feel the silence.

Please note

When performing this dynamic dancing meditation, allow the shaking to come to you naturally. Don't force it. You should stand in silence, let loose and feel it coming. You can help your body slightly, when it starts trembling on its own, but don't make it happen forcibly. You must enjoy its blissful feeling, welcome it, facilitate it, accept it, but not will it.

Forcing this shaking will turn it into an exercise at a physical level. Then, even though you'll shake, it'll happen merely on the surface. The experience will not be penetrative, and you'll continue with the rocklike stiff and solid existence within.

You can employ through the nose breathing as explained in the Phase I of the Active meditation chapter. This will help with the trembling.

This shaking, when it happens naturally will shake the very foundations of your being, melting you from inside. When it happens on its own, allow it; you'll become the shaking and let it take over.

CHAPTER 6 - MEDITATING WITH HUMMING AND HANDS

No, this meditation isn't what you're thinking it to be! ☺ This method normally lasts for one hour and features 3 different stages. It works best when performed during the early morning hours. Nevertheless, you can practice it at any time of the day, either alone or in others' company. However, it's important to do it empty stomach and stay inactive for a minimum of 15 minutes after its completion.

It involves a sitting position, wherein a humming sound and certain hand movements are made, resulting in creation of an inner balance, or harmonization of the mind and body.

HOW TO DO IT?

Making your body vibrate through humming here is key. It is this vibration that will get you in a meditative state. As mentioned above, this meditation technique involves 3 different stages as follows:

STAGE I – HUMMING (30 MINUTES)

Look for a place where you can perform this meditation peacefully. Sit down in a relaxed manner.

Now close your eyes and press your lips together. Slowly start making a humming sound, loud enough to be heard by people in your surroundings. It'll create a vibrating effect throughout your body. The humming sound can be made better by visualizing an empty vessel or some hollow tube, filled with nothing but the humming vibrations.

Soon, you'll reach a point when the humming sound will happen on its own, with you turning into the listener. Please note, this method involves no special breathing technique - you're allowed to move your body or change the humming sound's pitch slowly and steadily if you like.

Stage II – Hand movements (15 minutes)

This stage is further subdivided into 2 distinct sections of 7 ½ minutes each. It should be done only after having gone through the Humming stage.

Section 1

During the first half, you're required to move your palms and hands upwards, in a sort of outward circular motion. Start at the navel point and move both your hands upward, thereafter dividing them in a way that they make two big circles, mirroring each other on the right and left side.

Please ensure that the movement is kept as slow as possible; so slow that you don't feel it happening at all. Visualize sending out energy to the entire universe.

Section 2

After around 7 ½ minutes of completing such motion, you must bring your palms and hands down, and then start their motion in the opposite direction. This time, the hands will come close to each other at the navel point, and then divide from each other in the outward direction, towards the sides of your body.

You must visualize as if you're taking lots of energy from the universe into your body. Energy is everywhere. There is energy even in an empty space. Imagine harnessing this energy from your surroundings and from the universe. Don't inhibit any slow and soft body movements, if you feel like.

Stage III – The stillness (15 minutes)

In this stage, you must lie down or sit in an absolutely still and quiet manner.

Notice that in almost every meditation method there is some variation of The stillness stage. That's because this stage is very important and should not be looked over.

The couples' variation

This type of humming and hands meditation can even be practiced by couples together. Both the partners must sit opposite to each other, with their bodies covered with nothing but a plain bed sheet (Sounds tempting! But don't go there yet!). Hold each other's hands in a crossed manner.

The room must be lit by nothing other than 4 small candles, and perhaps some nice smelling incense that's going to be used only for this particular meditation technique.

Now, with your eyes closed, start making that humming sound explained in the stage I. Continue humming for the recommended 30 minutes. Soon you'll both experience the energies from your bodies meeting together through vibration, merging into and uniting with each other.

Performing this meditation on a regular basis will help you connect better to your inner self as well as to your spouse (when done with a partner).

Chapter 7 - Sitting Meditation

If you give it a thought, sitting still is actually one of the most difficult tasks. But once you get the knack of it, by practicing it on a regular basis, you can easily perform sitting meditation for at least a few hours each day.

When you do this meditation, many things will start happening gradually on their own. You may feel sleepy, dreamy and may even hallucinate. Several thoughts may start crowding your mind. To top it all, your mind may also reason why are you idling away your time this way?! You could've easily earned some extra money, watched a movie, attended a concert or even gossiped with friends! There are so many things you could've done! Your mind will try its best to force you out of your meditative state.

The trick lies in perseverance. Soon a day will come when you'll no longer feel sleepy and the mind won't feel tired. Rather, it'll surrender to you. There'll be no disturbing thoughts, dreams or hallucinations.

You'll be able to just sit there and do nothing at all! During this state, everything becomes silence and the peaceful feeling is absolutely blissful. When you reach this state, you'll experience the touch of something that can only be described as divine, something to do with the power of universe.

How to do it?

Sit in some comfortable place, facing a blank wall almost an arm's length away. Your eyes should neither be closed, nor completely open. Rather, half open, good enough to rest a soft gaze on the wall.

Keep your back as straight as possible. One of your hands should be inside the other, with both thumbs touching each other and forming an oval shape.

Sit still in this position at least for 30 minutes. Avoid directing your attention anywhere else. Stay alert and receptive, allowing only choice-less awareness to stay with you.

Points you should take care of

Firstly, this type of meditation can be practiced anywhere, but make sure that whatever you look at isn't too exciting. For instance, the things in front of you shouldn't move so much, that they end up becoming a distraction.

Perhaps you can watch trees, as they're always still. You may even watch upwards, towards the sky, unless there's a lot of activity happening up there! Or just sit in one corner of your room, facing a wall.

Secondly, avoid looking at any particular point. Your focus should be on nothing but <u>emptiness</u>. Avoiding concentrating or focusing on anything can provide a very relaxing feeling.

Thirdly, make sure that your breathing is relaxed, which means that it should happen naturally without you needing to force it.

The fourth point is keeping your body immobile, as much as possible. Try finding a good posture in the beginning itself. You can take help of a mattress and/or pillow, but once you're comfortable, avoid any movement. This is because the only way to silence the mind is by silencing the body, which can't happen if you move constantly. After all, body and mind are one.

This meditation may seem slightly difficult initially, but will become tremendously enjoyable once you get a hang of it.

Conclusion

If you've arrived on this page after diligently reading through all the chapters, and applying some or all of the meditation ways explained herein, you're well set on your way to still your mind, hear the voice of your intuition and trust your heart! Now choose the meditation methods that suit you best and practice them regularly. Then all you need to do is stay disciplined about the meditation routine that you've chosen for yourself.

Note that some of the meditation methods described here were not meant to be done everyday, especially the intense ones like Active meditation, Whirling meditation and Dynamic Dancing meditation. Other methods on the other hand, like Sitting or Breathing meditation can be practiced everyday. It's best to choose a couple of methods and practice them at your own convenience, but with the necessary discipline.

See what works best for you and make it a part of your life. Let the meditation become your habit.

You might've noticed that I'm a big advocate of the Active meditation. In my opinion it's the fastest way of meditating to get the maximum benefits. You will become a better, more self-aware version of you after only one session.

If you become good at it you will learn to feel your way through life. This applies to any other meditation method as well.

These were some of the best meditation practices I've tried so far and have received an amazing value from them. I have no doubts that they will benefit you too greatly if you apply them in your life.

Lastly, I want to sincerely thank you for reading this book. I hope you received some value from it. If you did please consider leaving a review. It helps more people find this book.

All the best!

Nicolas Knoll

Printed in Great Britain
by Amazon.co.uk, Ltd.,
Marston Gate.